To lucia,

My daughter of
dubious origins. I think
She is a robot! I never see her eating
lots of love Does She run on
Batteries?

love Michael

DAVID HOLLOWELL

DAVID HOLLOWELL

TEXT BY
SEYMOUR HOWARD

PUBLISHED BY
JOHN NATSOULAS PRESS

Front Cover: *Picasso Revisited,*1991, pastel on paper, 48" x 68"

John Natsoulas Press
140 F Street
Davis, California, 95616
(916) 756-3938
FAX (916) 756-3961

Pre-Press The California Aggie, Davis
Produced by Printech, Honolulu
Printed and Bound in Hong Kong

TABLE OF CONTENTS

Self Portrait
1984

ARTIST'S STATEMENT

David Hollowell's work is pretty spectacular. The thing I admire in his work is its ambition, the interesting problems he sets for himself. He takes on really complex painterly issues, such as the attempt to distinguish between size and scale within them. And the fact that he works with the figure is a kind of heroic challenge.

Wayne Thiebaud
ARTnews, November 1991

Let me start this description of my development from the time I was in graduate school. The very first painting I did in grad school was a self portrait. When unsure of what to paint, paint a self portrait. Seemed like the logical thing to do. After the first critique of that self portrait, I realized I was in a little over my head. You see, I thought it would be enough just to impress them with my talent, my ability to render, to replicate. Turned out I was dead wrong. They were way past being impressed by that high school trickery. They wanted more. Well, I still didn't know what to do so I painted a still life, again trying to paint what I set up, what I saw. Same criticism, but I heard it a little clearer this time.

To make a two-year stint in grad school into a few sentences, what I did was figure out a way to teach myself how to develop the language of form. I did not paint the figure again while in grad school. No reason to; I had to figure out how to make a floor meet a wall, how to get a bowl to sit on a table. I was now looking for more than mere replication; I was looking for an experience, a felt experience. The paintings I did during this time were all rather small, nothing larger than 35 inches or so. The figure was too loaded with baggage that I clearly was unable to carry.

After graduation I left New Haven for St. Louis, and left much of my life behind. It was time for a new beginning. No reason to make the the same paintings; no reason I should keep the figure out any longer. I figured I had paid my dues. I'd invested two years into developing a language; well, now it was time to use it. The first painting I did in my new environment incorporated the human figure. It has been the one common subject in all my work since.

Let me tell you one of the most important lessons I learned while studying at Yale. It was the lesson on learning how to simplify the seemingly complex nature of painting. Primarily, I learned that until one consciously identifies and understands the picture plane and its relevance to image making, one can never move past its formidable surface. Over my two-year stint in grad school, I developed several methods by which I could effectively stay in touch with the idea of picture plane. I taught myself how to see the world around me as a flat, two-dimensional surface. Kind of reversing the roles, if you get my gist. The world around me was the subject for painting; all I had to do was start seeing it as a painting, seeing it as a flat surface, realizing that it was all an illusion. In order to do this I developed these elaborate string grids that I would set up in front of my view and would plot the world I saw directly on an adjacent gridded canvas. I also taught myself how to draw directly on glass. To be specific, I would look out my window and actually draw what I saw directly on the glass, realizing that

the glass was the picture plane. It was flat. Drawing that which I saw on the glass simply affirmed this point. I would then elaborate on these skeletal drawings until I had my desired experience.

After grad school I continued this process of using the window device and the string grid until I decided to experiment with the camera obscura. This proved to be yet another useful tool in assisting me to develop my understanding of the nature of picture plane. I don't want to bore you with cluttered details on how this device was used; suffice it to say that I could see the world on that flat opaque ground glass which is the viewing screen. By drawing directly on this screen, I was once again abstracting the three-dimensional world to two dimensions. I remember using this device for a year or so before I realized enough was enough. Why should I spend my time only identifying the looks of the world I lived in? Why should I merely imitate the light of nature as it shined through windows onto objects and walls in these interiors I inhabited? There was one series of images I was working on at the time that focused on a woman standing by a window. It was first designed by using the camera obscura. After several variations on the theme, I realized that if I eliminated the window, I could avoid merely illustrating light in my painting. I could actually make the pigment itself be the light. A whole new concept arose. There was no going back. I was at that time aware of the fact that I was on my own; I was in uncharted territory. It was a feeling of fright, but also wonderful enlightenment. I no longer had need of my precious devices. They could not help me now.

Well, as is always the case when concept is altered, so too is technique. I could no longer technically paint the same way. It was at this time, about 1979 or 1980, that I first used pastels. It seemed the logical thing to do at the time. I had no hang–ups as to the right or wrong way to use these things. All I knew was that their color was pure. It was pure, raw, intense pigment. These pastels had their own light. I remember feeling extremely liberated by their directness. Two things started happening simultaneously at this time. I was starting to invent my images more, and was also starting to increase the size of the picture plane.

Up to this point, drawing for me was either that thing that I did on Wednesday night at some art school with fellow artists, sharing the costs of a model, or that which I did on the paper or canvas to design the underlying structure of an endurance piece. I was by now playing around with pastel sticks, and began to see how by cross hatching a network of woven color I could build my forms, my space, and my light. So I instinctively tried using charcoal and graphite in the same manner. At first it didn't work. I was still unclear as to what drawing meant to me, how I could use it, why I should use it. It wasn't until I picked up some prismacolor pencils that I finally made a bit

of a connection. Using these pencils, I methodically built up my images as I was doing in pastel and paint. What I was beginning to realize was that if I could stay in touch with the concept of form as I was starting to understand it, I could mold anything into my vision. As long as the vision was clear, all I had to do was keep beating at the technique until it yielded results. This, then, may explain to those of you who think that I'm merely a technician, one who delights only in crafting his pieces, one whose technique is merely a means to an end; technique is for me never an end in itself. I employ it in order to achieve my conceptual goals. So, whoever either enjoys or rejects my work only on technical competence is clearly missing the point. No one could sustain an image for as long as I do merely to entertain themselves with technique. If I can't get engaged or find myself believing in the illusions I'm creating, then there is no magic, no mystery. I'll go to whatever end I have to (technically) in order to have an experience. There can be no short cuts, no easy outs. I'm way too bull-headed for that.

In 1981 I spent a year in Roswell, New Mexico, on an artist–in–residence program. During this year I had the opportunity to explore some of these newly formed concepts. Given that the grant supplied me with a large studio and bought all of my materials, I could make no excuses. So I started putting the paint on thicker, with no medium. I started working even larger. You see, what happened was that as I was beginning to see the inherent "realness" in the pastels, I could not figure out how to equate this to oil paint. What I could not get was the matteness, the flatness of the hue in oils that I was naturally getting in pastels. Coming from a traditional oil glaze technique in painting to a matte flat surface was not an easy accomplishment. I required this matteness because I could not stand looking at these larger images with all their reflections that occurred due to the glossiness of the glaze or medium.

I completed a lot of paintings over that year. These paintings certainly had their shortcomings, but they were an integral link in assisting me with my developing concepts. I intentionally made the interiors sparse. I did not want to spend an inordinate amount of time building interior forms within the central or overall form of the painting. Several of these works were mural in size, 20 by 11 feet.

After the year in Roswell, I worked at trying to enter the real world of bills and expenses, deadlines and commitments. It was rather difficult, but I was saved again from the real world. I received another grant, this time to the Netherlands for a year. What luck, two years of unadulterated time; an artist's dream come true. Perhaps I can best explain my character by telling you that I spent this year working on drawings (graphite) that never got any bigger than 12 inches in any given dimension. These drawings clarified for me the dilemma I was having between technique and concept. These small, tightly woven cross–hatched graphite drawings showed me how to make the connection I was missing. They were the first works I did which consciously tried to create a harmony between figure and ground, that spoke from the same voice. Somehow I felt I got a handle on the concept of organic unity, or the totality of form itself.

I was hired at Davis the following year. The knowledge I gained from making these drawings has entertained me ever since. It's as though I'm now somewhat like I was upon leaving grad school; I'm liberated, more free to explore possibilities of image than ever before. Perhaps this explains the more complex situations that I am developing in my subject matter these days. Perhaps this explains why I'm building my own "chapel," so to speak. But that is the subject for another book; suffice it to say that my interest in image making is as alive and well as it has ever been. Come and see my chapel if you're ever in Woodland.

David Hollowell
Woodland, California, January, 1993

Untitled, 1981, prismacolor on paper, 24" x 36"

DAVID HOLLOWELL AND HIS DRAWINGS

SEYMOUR HOWARD

On first view—the best view—we admire the work of David Hollowell for its achievements in imagination and execution. These are what the Greeks called *phantasia* (bringing to light) and *techne* (*facture*, or making), attributes that they identified in work that we call "art," a concept for which their oh–so–highly inflected language had no word (the closest is *poesis*, poetry). For them, sublimated illusionism was an integral part of life, as it is for David Hollowell.

When I first saw Dave's work, including several intricately finished drawings, in 1984, he was a candidate to become a member of our faculty of artists at Davis. The distinguished jury that invited him to join them, and to stay, included Robert Arneson, Roy de Forest, Manuel Neri, Roland Peterson, and Wayne Thiebaud, among others. As an art historian, I immediately saw—and David quickly concurred—that he drew on a complex background of art historical imagery and method. His is the way of a recent generation of eclectic post-Modernist artists, who participate in the democratization of masterpieces and their means from every period and region of art, combining them with contemporary imagery and meanings.

His works are of the moment and episodic, like the juxtaposed television-based imagery of David Salle, and they are meticulous and art historical, like the compositions of another young American, Mark Tansey, or the Italian Carlo Maria Mariani. But David Hollowell is more gentle, circumspect, and autobiographical than they, in the manner of a lyric contemporary Pointillist.

Arched Room with Frescos (Jim on Left), 1987, pastel on paper, 60" x 84"

The Seamstress, 1979, oil on canvas, 24" x 24"

The *metier* of master, apprentice, and studio, an abiding system of training and production in pre–Modern traditions of painting, is now broken. It was replaced in the age of social, industrial, and technological revolution by courses of study and research in academies and universities and by learning in the public collections of museums and galleries. Masterworks of illusionism, now popularized in the photo–engravings of proliferating art books and reproduced (like their mimetic descendants) in even more numerous magazines, snapshots, films, videos, and television appearances, constitute a ubiquitous array of pre-digested imagery instantaneously available to everyone— not only professional painters and their patron–collectors. Hollowell's work reflects these conditions.

As professionals know and have known for centuries, artists learn more from art and from each other than from nature. For them (and us), chaos is partly tamed by the comprehending views of their predecessors, and contemporaries.

Artists have often enlisted aspects of famous old and new art styles and images, synthesizing them with selected and personally charged representations that have private and broadly–based contemporary significance. This process is Eclecticism, what the Greeks called "choosing the best of the best," in the service of the maker and viewer. Such eclectic practice, an Ancient as well as Modern approach to the arts, characterizing the work of academics, is ultimately descended from traditions fostered in the original Academy—the philosopher Plato's school of ideas and ideals, which the Greeks called "forms," the reality underlying appearance.

Old masters?! I find them to be good teachers.
—Hollowell

As a boy and adolescent in rural New York state, Hollowell (b. 1951) aspired to be a commercial artist until visits to art museums inspired him to want to become a modern Vermeer, to join the "Old Masters," whose paintings and sculptures enchant him. He emulates and reproduces their works in a venerable *paragone* (acknowledgment and competition) of comparisons and juxtapositions.

Hollowell received an eclectic training in the noted art school at Yale, where the abstracting still–life and landscape painter William Bailey had an especially strong influence on him. At Yale he was something of a maverick, working on problems of illusionism in a seemingly conservative way, presenting life–like figures and objects in a carefully constructed space, represented on its antithesis, the flat picture plane.

After graduation (1976), work at several teaching posts, and a stay as artist in residence in New Mexico, he went to Holland on a fellowship, to study Baroque masters of naturalism, whose realist, materialist, and intimist paintings were closest to his deepest interests. He has further developed these interests with his colleagues and students at Davis.

Johannes Vermeer, *The Lace–Maker*, canvas, 9.5"x 8.25", Louvre, Paris

Hollowell's paintings dating from his stay in Holland (accompanied by precise preliminary drawings) are life–size and over–scale contemporary scenes, usually interiors. They are executed in oil and encaustic, an Ancient colorful wax technique that has been periodically revived, usually in

Time and Space, 1989, oil on masonite, 30" x 80"

combination with oil painting, from Baroque to Modern times, most recently with good effect by Jasper Johns. The compositions continue to be mostly figures in interiors or before architectural façades, variously framed and rendered on both large and miniature scales.

From the outset, Hollowell has been a slow and meticulous worker, describing his subjects with a jewel–like precision that demands long and sustained execution. Each figure, each element, while serving as a detail for the whole, is a gem of demanding vision and controlled execution on both a monumental and a miniaturist level, whatever the size of the piece. Because this self–limited production is very attractive, it is much in demand.

Drawings?! They ARE my paintings! I'm doing the same thing. They serve an array of purposes.

—Hollowell

Until now, Hollowell's drawings, which are an integral part of his working process, have not been shown *en bloc.*

Like his paintings, the drawings, often ancillary or preparatory studies, occasionally represent bits of landscape and architectural framework and furniture, but from the first they deal primarily with figures, always the most seductive yet difficult subject to make convincing and satisfying.

Drawings usually record an artist's first thoughts or early assays and give an intimate view into the making and perception of more formally finished works prepared for public display. Drawing, what the Italians call *disegno*, reveals the thinking that goes into the components and underlying structure of compositions. These ideas are often further developed in painting or in more advanced sketches of a composition and its details. So drawing is an arena for achieving control and understanding. It is basic to Academy training and its approaches to art, as well as being a genre of intimate exhibition work.

During the nineteenth century and after, many Academy artists worked exclusively in drawing before beginning painting, to achieve mastery of their craft. The magical realist–naturalist Caspar David Friedrich, for example, a similarly obsessed and mystical observer of art and of nature, did not paint in oils until he was 30 years old. In varying degrees of finish, drawings and sketches underlie virtually all ambitious painting from pre–Renaissance to Modern times, up until the revolutionary technique of direct, outdoor (*plein air*) painting on white canvas introduced by the Impressionists.

The Drawing Room, 1985, gouache on paper, 14" x 17"

Hollowell's masterful drawings illustrate a wide spectrum of approaches to and uses of drawing. For the initiate as well as the amateur, it is informative to identify the visual and technical sources that inspire and flavor his various sketches and give us an intimate view into his methods.

Hollowell's contouring outline drawings—recalling Renaissance studies of detail and of perspective by Ucello, Piero della Francesca, Leonardo, or Raphael revived by Modern academicians in the generation of Ingres, the Nazarenes, and the pre-Raphaelites—usually record the final or penultimate scaffolding and decisions about particular elements, to be finished in paintings filled in with color and tone or in more worked-up sketches.

His drawings with delicately modeled outline and shading particularly resemble works in silverpoint or other metal points by Renaissance artists and their modern Neoclassic and Academic re-interpreters. Broad and heavy, more tentative, reworked outline sketches, frequently softened with hatchings and other modulations, recall the more painterly and reductive techniques of later artists, from the time of Degas and Cézanne to Balthus, Maillol, and Kitaj, who often prepared such sketches for gallery presentation.

Hollowell's drawings with extensive penciled hatchings (sometimes repeated in erasures) closely resemble graphic works by the *Scuola Metafisica* painter Giorgio Morandi, and older sketches by Renaissance painters and sculptors that create effects of broken light and a rounded modeling of forms. Hollowell's networks of dark and light hatching make gradients of tone that also bring to mind the spots and patches of modern Tachist and Macchiaioli-like compositions in watercolor, oil, and printmaking from the time of early Romantics like Goya and Turner to early twentieth-century Intimists of the School of Paris like

Bonnard or Vuillard, or Sickert, from London's Camden School. His densely intricate drawings of this type, usually executed with pencils of varying degrees of hardness, echo and prefigure his "painterly" manner, which employs minute gradients in tone and chroma.

Drawings in which the above techniques are combined, brought to their highest finish, and ultimately colored in the pure dry pigments of pastel (a medium introduced by Venetian Renaissance colorists), most resemble Hollowell's paintings in detail and, in some cases, their life–like scale. In general effect, the most densely finished sketches recall Seurat's velvet scribbling with dark chalks and graphite over pebbled paper, and his Pointillist spots of color in paintings, overlaid with adjacent strokes of pure pigment in a miniaturist polychrome of smoky "sfumato." That effect Hollowell also simulates with a web of hatchwork and an extended vocabulary of other "greying" linear calligraphic strokes used by Modern graphic artists working with pencil, pen, and etching needle.

His final post–Impressionist Pointillist techniques resemble most the work of French Intimists, where tone and chroma, made literally plastic in strokes, also help make the figure seem round, palpable, resonating, and alive.

Mother and Child, 1989, pastel on paper, 96" x 80"

Painting?! For me, painting is a living art. When I first saw a fresco by Piero I saw life. Those images were alive for me.

Perimeters?! Perspectives?! They are crucial—vessels for and affirmations of the work. I never tire of the magic I feel when I can enter the space I created.

—Hollowell

As noted, Hollowell's works incorporate a broad spectrum of sources, taken from what André Malraux once wittily

Georges Seurat, 1883-84, oil on canvas, The National Gallery, London

identified as our "museum without walls," a history of art in picture books that incorporate millennia of examples.

His paintings and his drawings for them abound with references to canonical art images and their makers. These are his models and competition. In the nineteenth century they became icons, saints, and heroes for the Moderns, in and outside of the profession; the giant stars of culture, from Giotto and Donatello to Leonardo, Raphael, and Michelangelo, had been idolized since the time of Vasari.

At Davis, Hollowell often teaches an introductory course dealing with the principles and, more tangentially, the history of art. His text is E. H. Gombrich's *Story of Art.* What better source for art and ideas than the essays and images written and selected by that great explainer of the compulsion toward illusionism characterizing Ancient and Modern masters? Illusionism—the abstracting and variously textured simulation of objects and figures in space, light, and atmosphere—attempts to represent perception and appearance for the beholder and for the communal eye. This man–made likeness, a "reality" or "realism" with its own "realities," introduces multivalent issues of identification and crisis in definitions of "reality," in what recent French Existentialists have ambiguously addressed as *réalité*. These matters are both informative about and symptomatic of Hollowell's basic interests, training, and background.

The Galleria, 1985, oil an masonite, 120" x 240"

Cardinal to his work is the handling of light as a pervasive, unifying, principle. Depicting direct and reflected light helps to model and to place the figure and objects accurately in the picture's constructed space, which he meticulously fashions with an implied or expressed gridwork used to open and to diagram the picture plane (also reflected in the measured application of drawn or painted strokes on its flat surface).

The serious play in identifying and using honored visual sources in new contexts for personal and communal ends—an Academic device since Antiquity, revived in the

Interior with Eight Figures #6, 1984, graphite on paper, 6" x 15"

Classicizing Renaissance and by Mannerists and Baroque Eclectics—continues in Academic traditions to the present day. In the era of the sound bite, the television remote control, short–term profit–taking, fast food, and the lust for instant gratification accompanying recent decades of self–indulgent narcissism, the kaleidoscopic self–serving selections from our visual treasure–house that are enlisted and illustrated by post–Modernists are a singularly apt reflection of and instruction for our times. Among them, Hollowell's muted ensembles, in tone, point of view, and execution, are singularly benign.

A casual list of Academic references in his work, in a quiz game of identification, would include pieces by (and portraits of) Poussin, Reni, Piero della Francesca, Raphael, Del Sarto, the Bellinis, Picasso, Masaccio, Van Gogh, Hopper, Donatello, Cézanne, Seurat, Balthus, De Hooch, Vermeer, Rodin, Ingres, Stella, Tooker, Puvis de Chavannes, and the Classical masters of Stabia, the Venus de' Medici, and other antiquities.

Hollowell's work can be viewed as a collage or collation of prints, paintings, photos, drawings, slides, and reproductions from that museum without walls comprised of the Old Masters. He incorporates the images into a stage-set sort of architecture that dramatizes an eclectic aggregate of associations: family and friends become one with old masters and their masterworks in dream halls fusing the hallowed and the commonplace. Somewhat like the sculptor Dwayne Hanson's life-like and everyday actors, they populate an idiosyncratically reconstituted museum of the history of art, where intimate familiars— wife, children, parents, self, and friends, wearing sneakers, leotards, bermuda shorts, and pedal pushers—engage, as worthy subjects and witnesses, in a venerable genre of mute "sacred conversation" with the great masters or their ghosts before and within walls displaying their works.

We see Terry, the artist's wife and recurrent model, the *anima*-complement of desire and fulfillment, in ever-changing manifestations: the aging mother and father, as well as the children; the active, working, watching basket-shooter painter; and a bevy of friends, associates, onlookers, and artists, accompanied by resurrections of Cézanne, Poussin, Picasso, and company. We find our contemporaries seated in Dutch interiors or standing and moving in Italian Renaissance and post-Modernist spaces— perennial Western cubicles—recast and set into concocted gallery and chapel halls within multiple frames that condense and expand into allusions to illusionism in a

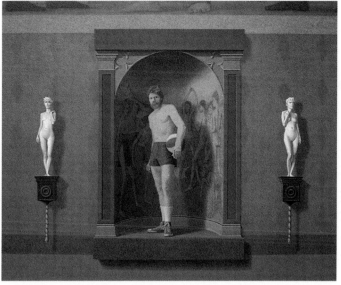

The Artist as a Basketball Player, 1988, oil on masonite, 78" x 96"

magic man-made universe of compounded interiors with "loaded" yet dissolving boundaries.

Viewing and re-viewing the works is like a quick flip through the story of art—a collage or frieze of favorite images fused into an aggregate dream of interiors with permuting walls and frames that break into each other and the exhibition space and enter into life itself, much like exterior and interior aspects of the viewer's space or mind. These structures can be viewed metaphorically as analogues for interior journeys or flights into self-referential, personal,

Adam and Eve Soliloquy, 1987, pastel on paper, 90" x 112"

context and by the maker's hand and selection, are nonetheless accurately re–presented in their details.

Like altar pieces, Hollowell's compositions present a timely and timeless aggregate of still, but affectively charged, subject–referents in a shared space, eliciting latent, implicit, and dimly understood responses and actions. These are the components of audience in–put prerequisite for Ancient and Modern heroic epics of narration and meaning. The works, for all their high finish, are ultimately completed by the observer. As with the pediment of Zeus at Olympia, the actions and meanings of the statuesque figures are to be understood in epic–episodic fashion, but with Hollowell's work, at a more preconscious level. His cast of characters, which often echo their mural and sculpture reflections, are largely vehicles for silent unarticulated emotion, and for identification by association and empathy with an epic of past, present, and future views of life.

idiosyncratic worlds, which, by extension, become universal, archetypal visions that function like message–capsules. As with objects in still–lifes, they are "real" and naturalist reflections on vanity, recalling the Ecclesiates "vanity of vanities," the only life we have, need, and may enjoy.

The references to Hollowell's sources in art and nature, like the spaces, are both shallow and deep. The images, synthesized into a new realm and transformed by their

In Hollowell's drawings and paintings, expression resides mainly in the execution and its formal qualities. The artist as a person is naturally reflected in his work and signature: gentle, soft–spoken, unassuming, hard–working, good natured, dedicated, committed, and a zealous purist with a Virgo–like innocence yet healthy heterosexual eroticism, a resolved master of forms with the open edge of a homespun yet delicate sensitivity. David Hollowell is a subtle professional working in a contemporary space–time warp, a steady and ultimately outgoing introvert. In modern dress and undress, his work is visually analogous in form and temperament to the toy and evanescent, yet intensive, aspects of Van Eyck, Terborch, or Seurat. A quiet, almost contemplative, sadness pervades the imagery, with its Surrealistically silent spaces and figures—which complements the light and joyous color.

In whole and in part, Hollowell's works reflect a labor of love and obsession—a tender loving care, exacting, observing, fondling, stroking, making the objects subjects of desire that radiate an aura, an aroma, of possession...and its opposite, abstracting distance. The much–lived–in work, with its sacrifice and celebration, is regularly and readily admired by viewers. It is a success, locally and nationally; it reflects and elicits whole spectrums of possession.

Master Model Maker (The Set Painter), 1988, pastel on paper, 55" x 69"

The images, as compounded records of perception, doing, and making, are what poetry is about, by definition, according to the Greeks, and what life means. As such, the drawings and paintings are replications and records of the human condition, and in them, as in all things (if you've an eye to see), is the recognition and the solace, the joy and the epiphany, of what it is to be alive. Hollowell's works show, again, that there is no break or difference between art and life. They illustrate the understanding of what it is to be alive and doing. As the Ancients knew, and as Socrates (and Goethe) said: *We are our actions; that is our teaching. Know thy self.*

Davis, California, December 1992

DAVID HOLLOWELL

PLATES

DAVID HOLLOWELL

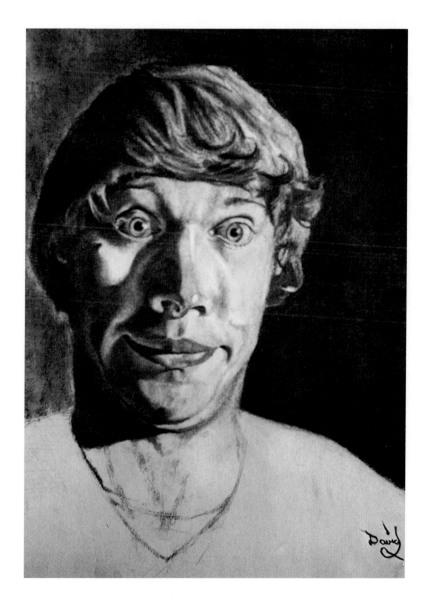

PLATE 1
Gesture
1973

PLATE 2
Untitled
1976

PLATE 3
Untitled
1976

PLATE 4
Untitled
1976

PLATE 5
Untitled
1976

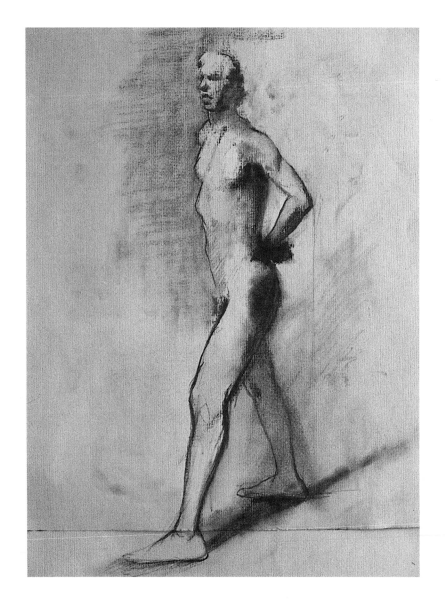

PLATE 6
Untitled
1976

PLATE 7
Untitled
1976

PLATE 8
Untitled
1980

PLATE 9
Untitled
1980

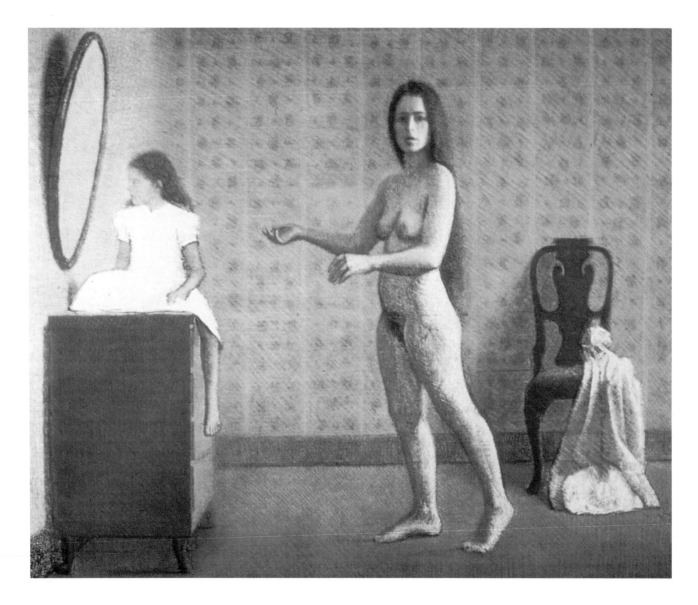

PLATE 10
Untitled
1980

PLATE 11
The Blue Pitcher
1981

PLATE 12
Untitled
1981

PLATE 13
Untitled
1981

PLATE 14
Untitled
1981

PLATE 15
Figure Study
1980

PLATE 16
Conversation Study #1
1982

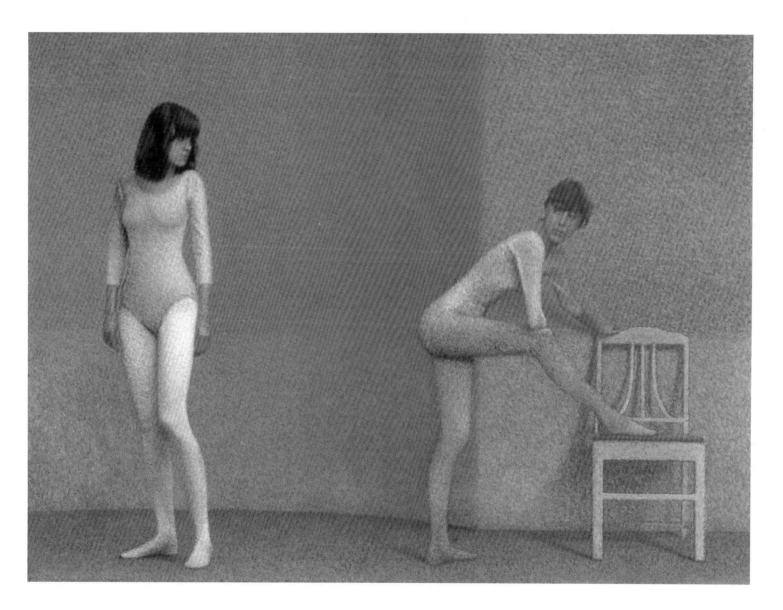

PLATE 17
Interior with Two Figures #11
1984

PLATE 18
Interior with Eight Figures #8
1985

PLATE 19
La Galleria
1985

PLATE 20
Two Figures with Blue Ladder
1985

PLATE 21
Arched Room with Frescos (Jim on Left)
1987

PLATE 22
Master Model Maker (The Set Painter)
1988

PLATE 23
Adam and Eve Soliloquy
1988

PLATE 24
Grey Space: Dave
1988

PLATE 25
Grey Space: Terry
1988

PLATE 26
Grey Space: Loie
1988

PLATE 27
Untitled
1989

PLATE 28
Time and Space
1989

PLATE 29
Mother and Child
1989

PLATE 30
Picasso Revisited
1991

PLATE 31
Fading Images
1989

PLATE 32
Conversation
1991

PLATE 33
Interior with Two Figures #3
1984

PLATE 34
Interior with Eight Figures #6
1984

PLATE 35
Drawing Room
1985

PLATE 36
The Arch
1986

PLATE 37
Atrium with Jug and Screen
1986

PLATE 38

Opera
1986

PLATE 39
Atrium with Jug and Screen
1987

PLATE 40
Morandi Revisited
1988

PLATE 41
The Dreamer
1988

PLATE 42
Study of Artist and Family
1989

PLATE 43
Architectural Interior Study
1990

PLATE 44
Interior with Model, Table and Potted Plant
1990

PLATE 45
Foster and Hannah
1990

PLATE LIST

1. *Gesture*
1973, charcoal on paper
18" x 26".

2. *Untitled*
1976, charcoal on paper
25" x 22"

3. *Untitled*
1976, charcoal on paper
20" x 24".

4. *Untitled*
1976, charcoal on paper
25" x 22".

5. *Untitled*
1976, charcoal on paper
22" x 20".

6. *Untitled*
1976, charcoal and pencil on paper
30" x 26".

7. *Untitled*
1976, charcoal on paper
30" x 26".

8. *Untitled*
1980, pastel on paper
83" x 60".

9. *Untitled*
1980, pastel on paper
40" x 44".

10. *Untitled*
1980, pastel on paper
40" x 44".

11. *The Blue Pitcher*
1981, pastel on paper
40" x 44".

12. *Untitled*
1981, prismacolor on paper
24" x 36".

13. *Untitled*
1981, prismacolor on paper
30" x 36".

14. *Untitled*
1981, pencil on paper
22" x 30".

15. *Figure study*
1980, pastel on paper
12" x 10".

16. *Conversation Study #1*
1982, charcoal and pastel on paper
17" x 14".

17. *Interior with Two Figures #11*
1984, pastel on paper
40" x 53".

18. *Interior with Eight Figures #8*
1985, graphite on paper
12" x 24".

19. *La Galleria*
1985, oil and wax on masonite
120" x 240".

20. *Two Figures with Blue Ladder*
1985, pastel on paper
54" x 40".

21. *Arched Room with Frescoes*
(Jim on Left)
1987, pastel on paper
60" x 84".

22. *Master Model Maker
(The Set Painter)*
1988, pastel on paper
55" x 69".

23. *Adam and Eve Soliloquy*
1987, pastel on paper
90" x 112".

24. *Grey Space: Dave*
1988, pastel on paper
46" x 43".

25. *Grey Space: Terry*
1988, pastel on paper
46" x 43".

26. *Grey Space: Loie*
1988, pastel on paper
46" x 43".

27. *Untiltled*
1989, pastel on paper
18" x 12".

28. *Time and Space*
1990, oil on masonite
28" x 60".

29. *Mother and Child*
1989, pastel on paper
82" x 90".

30. *Picasso Revisited*
1991, pastel on paper
48" x 68".

31. *Fading Images*
1989, pastel on paper
96" x 78".

32. *Conversation*
1990, pastel on paper
68" x 53".

33. *Interior with Two Figures #3*
1984, graphite on paper
8" x 11".

34. *Interior with Eight Figures #6*
1984, graphite on paper
12" x 15".

35. *Drawing Room*
1985, gouache on paper
12" x 24".

36. *The Arch*
1986, graphite on paper
14" x 13".

37. *Atrium with Jug and Screen*
1986, graphite on paper
14" x 18".

38. *Opera*
1986, graphite on paper
12" x 24".

39. *Stage with Beams*
1987, graphite on paper
16" x 28".

40. *Morandi Revisited*
1988, graphite on paper
4 1/2" x 7 1/2".

41. *The Dreamer*
1988, graphite on paper
8" x 7".

42. *Study of Artist and Family*
1989, gouache on paper
4 1/2" x 7 1/2".

43. *Architectural Interior Study*
1990, graphite on paper
12 1/4" x 9".

44. *Interior with Model Table and
Potted Plant*
1990, gouache and pencil on paper
19" x 26".

45. *Foster and Hannah*
1990, graphite on paper
6" x 7".

CHRONOLOGY

1951
Born in Hornell, New York.

1973
Bachelor of Fine Arts, Ithaca College, New York, with various awards and an NCAA post-graduate scholarship.

1976
Master of Fine Arts with painting major and art history minor at Yale University, New Haven, Connecticut. Recipient of Elizabeth Confield Hicks Award (outstanding representational painter) at Yale University. Began as teaching assistant at Yale.

1976
Taught at Washington University, St. Louis, Missouri, for one year, where he met his future wife, Terry Cronan.

1977
Began as assistant professor at Fontbonne College, St. Louis, until 1980. Received a painting grant, Millay Colony for the Arts, Austerlitz, New York.

1978
Acquired Mean Lucy, a mixed-breed golden lab.

1981
Received one-year grant from Roswell Museum and Art Center, Roswell, New Mexico.

1982
Married Terry.

1983
Birth of daughter, Loie Holly. Acquired Fat Lucy, a mixed-breed golden lab. Visiting artist at Gustavus Adolphus College, St. Peter, Minnesota, teaching painting, drawing, printmaking, and 20th-century art history. Received Lusk Memorial Fellowship, a one-year painting grant which allowed him to work in the Netherlands.

1984
Assistant professor teaching painting, drawing, and art appreciation at the University of California, Davis.

1987
Birth of daughter, Lucia Jasmine.

1988
Received a Western States Art Federation (WESTAF) Drawing Award (catalog).

1989
Birth of daughter, Adrienne Rose.

1991
Chosen by Wayne Thiebaud for "Artists Choose Artists" in November ARTnews.

1992
Birth of son, Jack Henry. Acquired "Hank," terrier of dubious origins.

DAVID HOLLOWELL

SOLO EXHIBITIONS

1976
Paul Mellon Art Center, Wallingford, Connecticut.

1978
Fontbonne College Gallery, St. Louis.

1981
Schweig Gallery, St. Louis.

1982
Roswell Museum and Art Center, Roswell (catalog).

1983
Jane Haslem Gallery, Washington, D.C.
Schaefer Gallery, Gustavus Adolphus College, St. Peter.

1985
Brunswick Gallery, Missoula, Montana.
Jane Haslem Gallery, Washington, D.C. (catalog).

1989
Alexander Milliken Gallery, New York (catalog).

1990
"Drawings & Paintings," Pence Gallery, Davis.
"David Hollowell," Sangre de Cristo Arts and Conference
    Center, Pueblo, Colorado.

1992
Maxwell Davidson Gallery, New York.

1993
John Natsoulas Gallery, Davis.

DAVID HOLLOWELL

GROUP EXHIBITIONS

1976
MFA Thesis Exhibition, Yale University Gallery, New
    Haven.

1977
Marilyn Pearl Gallery, New York.
Steinberg Gallery, Washington University, St. Louis.

1979
University of North Carolina, Greensboro.

1980
Messing Gallery, St. Louis.

1985
"Cowton," Chan Elliot Gallery, Sacramento, California.
"25th Anniversary Exhibition," Jane Haslem Gallery,
    Washington, D.C..
Sacramento/Davis Interface, Richmond Art Center,
    Richmond, California.
"New Works/New Faculty, Paintings & Drawings," Nelson
    Gallery, UC Davis.
"American Painters: Realism Idealism," Jane Haslem
    Gallery, Washington, D.C. (catalog).

1986
"American Painters: Realism Idealism," Jane Haslem
    Gallery, Washington, D. C. (traveling).
"Second Sight: Biennial IV," San Francisco Museum of
    Modern Art, San Francisco, California.

Paule Anglim Gallery, San Francisco.
"American Drawings: Realism Idealism," Jane Haslem,
    Washington, D.C.
 "Komar & Melamid, Ann McCoy, David Hollowell,"
    Paule Anglim Gallery, San Francisco.

1987
"The Woodland Connection," Pence Gallery, Davis.
Hearst Gallery, St. Mary's College, Moraga, California.
"Paintings and Sculpture by Candidates for Art Awards,"
    American Academy and Institute of Arts and Letters,
    New York.
"Foreshadow," Jane Haslem Gallery, Washington, D.C.
"Artists for Amnesty," Exhibition and Benefit Auction,
    Davis.
"Three Decades of Art in Davis," Davis Art Center, Davis.
"Three Directions in Drawing," Hearst Art Gallery, Saint
    Mary's College, Moraga.

1988
"Portraits," Anchorage Museum of History and Art,
    Anchorage, Alaska (catalog).
"fan-fare, n. 1. Spectacular display," Jane Haslem Gallery,
    Washington, D.C.
"Consonance," Jane Haslem Gallery, Washington, D.C.
"Summer Exhibition—Gallery Artists," Alexander F.
    Milliken Inc., New York.
"Fall Exhibition—Gallery Artists," Alexander F. Milliken
    Inc., New York.

Faculty and Alumni Art Show, Natsoulas/Novelozo
Gallery, Davis.
Group Show, Natsoulas/Novelozo Gallery, Davis.

1989
"Influences III," Judith Weintraub Gallery, Sacramento.
"A.C.D.H.H.H.J.N.P.P.S.T.," Nelson Gallery, UC Davis.

1990
"Interpreting the Figure," Alexander Milliken Gallery,
New York.
"Regarding Art," Kohler Arts Center, Sheboygan,
Wisconsin.

"Hayes and Hollowell," Nicolaysen Art Museum, Casper,
Wisconsin.
"Excellence on Paper," Bakersfield Museum of Art,
Bakersfield, California.
"Figure Drawing Exhibition," Sierra College Library
Gallery, Rocklin, California.
"New Shows at the NIC!," Randy Hayes and David
Hollowell, Nicolaysen Art Museum, Casper.

1991
Maxwell Davidson Gallery, New York.

BIBLIOGRAPHY

Allen, Jane Addams. "A Touch of the Dutch in Hollowell Paintings." *The Washington Times*, April 28, 1983.

Baker, Kenneth. "Art on the Art World." *San Francisco Chronicle,* September 21, 1986.

Cilensek, Cynthia. "Different Styles at UC Davis." *The Daily Democrat,* October 5, 1989.

Dalkey, Victoria. "The Resulting Show? Past Imperfect." *The Sacramento Bee*, Sepember 28, 1986.

Ingram, Jan. *The Anchorage Times*, June 13, 1988.

Jones, Shirley. *The Daily Democrat,* October 19, 1989.

King, Mary. "Simplified Shapes by Hollowell." *St. Louis Post-Dispatch*, February 17, 1981.

Lewis, Jo Ann. "Classic Poses of Hollowell; The Artist's Still-Life Figures at Haslem." *Washington Post*, January 1985.

Lee, Anthony. "A Leap Into the Past." *Artweek,* May 17, 1990.

McColm, Del. "Enjoyable Art Offers History and Humor." *The Davis Enterprise*, October 16, 1986.

Morch, Al. "Looking Back." *San Francisco Examiner*, September, 1986.

Moyle, Marilyn. "Artists Differ, But Find Success in Realism." *The Davis Enterprise*, March 15, 1990.

Neill, Jeanne. "Resident Artist Program Unique." *Roswell (New Mexico) Daily Record*, August 8, 1982.

Nixon, Bruce. "David Hollowell." *Art of California*, vol. 3, no. 6. November, 1990.

Pitman, Lyman. "There's More to Hollowell Than Meets the Eye." *The Pueblo Chieftan*, July 1, 1990.

Rice, Nancy. "David Hollowell." *New Art Examiner*, March, 1981.

Schlesinger, Ellen. "UC Davis Adds a Pair of Artists to Its Faculty." *The Sacramento Bee*, November 3, 1984.

Smith, Jim. "Artist Profile," *The Daily Democrat*, November 27, 1989.

Van Proyen, Mark. "The Hieroglyphics of Ambivalence." *Artweek,* October 4, 1992.

"Paintings Within Paintings." *Washington Post*, April 23, 1983.

"Teaching Brings Hollowell back To Basics." *The Davis Enterprise*, September 26, 1985.

"The Human Condition: Davis Galleries Emphasize Variety of Life in Fall Exhibtions." *The Davis Enterprise*, October 17, 1985.

"David Hollowell," catalog for Jane Haslem Gallery, Washington D.C., 1985.

"Drawing on the Basics." *The Sacramento Bee*, April 27, 1986.

"American Drawings: Realism Idealism," catalog for Jane Haslem Gallery, Washington D.C., 1986.

"Portraits: Here's Looking At You," catalog from Anchorage Museum of History and Art, Anchorage, Alaska, 1988.

"15 Artists in Printmaking & Drawing," 1988 WESTAF/NEA Regional Fellowships for Visual Artists, Santa Fe, New Mexico.

"Positions of Influence." *The Sacramento Bee*, November 31, 1989.Review of exhibition at Pence Gallery. *The Davis Enterprise*, May 17, 1990:

"Artworks about Art." *Sheboygan Press*, June 10, 1990.

"Something Borrowed Makes an Art Exhibit," *Milwaukee Journal*, June 17, 1990.

"This 'Art' More Than Academic." *Milwaukee Sentinel*, July 20, 1990.

"California Currents: Artists Choose Artists," *ARTnews*, vol. 90, no. 9, November 1991.

ABOUT THE AUTHOR

Seymour Howard, Senior Professor of Art History and Archaeology at the University of California at Davis, works in many areas, including drawings, and is a specialist in perceptions of Classical art. His wide-ranging research appears in more than 200 publications (including several dozen books, monographs, and catalogs) and in over 100 professional lectures, including printed papers given at the Hermitage, the British Museum, the Louvre, the National Gallery in Washington, in Kyoto, and at major national and international art congresses and universities here and abroad. Professor Howard is also a sometime potter, painter, graphic artist, and calligrapher. He founded the ceramics studio at UC Davis; his works are exhibited locally and overseas and he occasionally publishes commentary on the work of his colleagues.

CREDITS

Design and Production
Mark Bullard, Tony Novelozo, Axiom Photo and Design

Photography
Mark Bullard, Tom McNeill,
Tony Novelozo, Axiom Photo and Design

Copy Edit
Rachel A. Wettergreen
Ilia Howard

Research and Compilation
Jo Chun, Jeannine Harris, John Natsoulas, Popi
Natsoulas, Deborah Pansby, Danielle Restaino

DAVID HOLLOWELL